Play the Game
Tennis

Play the Game

Tennis

Simon Lee

WARD LOCK

Half-title page: *One of the giants of women's tennis, Steffi Graf keeps her eyes firmly on the ball while serving*

Title page: *The irrepressible Boris Becker stretching to make the kind of shot most tennis players only ever dream about*

Above: *Michael Chang's speed and athleticism on court excite crowds all over the world*

Contents

Foreword

Tennis in Britain is going through one of its healthiest periods. Thanks to world superstars like Pete Sampras, Martina Hengis, Tim Henman and Greg Rusedski, British youngsters are taking up the sport in large numbers, in the hope of emulating their idols.

At grass roots level, these newcomers are being encouraged away from the friendly game in the local park and into the world of competitive tennis.

For so long we have lacked that essential competitive edge amongst our top players; of course we have had exceptions like Virginia Wade, Mark Cox and Buster Mottram, and now in Greg Rusedski and Tim Henman we have a match for top Americans and Europeans. Hopefully in the years to come, more young British tennis players will make the breakthrough into the top flight.

For those youngsters starting to develop their game there can be no finer starting place than this book in the *Play the Game* series. The book is comprehensive yet at the same time easy to read without getting too technical.

The history of the game is chronicled from the day Major

Clopton Wingfield developed his variation of tennis, which went under the rather weird and wonderful name of 'sphairistiké'. The game has come a long way since then and is now one of the world's leading sports. In terms of its commercial value, there are few to rival it.

If you have dreams of winning Wimbledon, or representing your country in the Davis Cup or Federation Cup, then you have to start somewhere, and reading and acting on the advice given in *Play the Game: Tennis* is a sound starting point.

After offering a fascinating history of the game, the book introduces you to the equipment needed to play the game, and its guide to tennis terminology is particularly useful. The rules of the game are detailed in a simple but comprehensive way, and for those rules that may need that extra bit of clarification the author has cleverly included a question-and-answer section called the 'Rules Clinic'.

The final section shows you how to play the game of tennis. Any youngster taking up the game for the first time will undoubtedly have his or her own hero and will try to mould their game on that particular player. But, before you can do that, you must master the basic arts of service, ground strokes and volleys. *Play the Game: Tennis* shows you how to play all these shots, and in a simple way. It gets you started with the basics: thereafter it is up to you. The more you play the better you will become, and the better you get the more you will start developing some of your own techniques and points of style.

No book can turn you into the world's number one player – that is up to you. *Play the Game: Tennis* can, however, start you on that road to the top, and it will certainly lead you to more success and enjoyment in a wonderful game.

David Lloyd

History & development of tennis

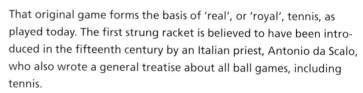

Tennis in its indoor form dates from the eleventh century, when a game called jeu de paume was played in French monasteries.

That original game forms the basis of 'real', or 'royal', tennis, as played today. The first strung racket is believed to have been introduced in the fifteenth century by an Italian priest, Antonio da Scalo, who also wrote a general treatise about all ball games, including tennis.

As an outdoor game, field tennis was mentioned in the English journal, *Sporting Magazine*, in 1793, when it was referred to as field tennis. This could well have been the same game as long tennis, which was mentioned in a *Book of Games and Sports* eighty years later.

Real, or royal, tennis was a game for the aristocracy, but lawn tennis, which became popular during Queen Victoria's reign, was a game for the middle class, who adapted real tennis into an outdoor game.

It is known that a Spaniard, J.B. Perera, and Major Harry Gem, clerk to the Birmingham Magistrates, played an outdoor version of tennis on the lawn of Perera's house in Ampton Road, Edgbaston, Birmingham, in 1859. They later played on a lawn adjacent to the Manor House Hotel, Leamington Spa, where, in 1872, along with Dr Frederick Haynes and Dr Arthur Tomkins, they formed the first known lawn tennis club, the Leamington Club. However, the sport was not called lawn tennis at the time but was referred to as either pelota or lawn rackets.

In 1874 Major Walter Clopton Wingfield attempted to commercialize the game, which he had now re-christened 'sphairistiké', by publishing a book of rules under the title *New and Improved Court for Playing the Ancient Game of Tennis*. Imagine Desmond Lynam on a Saturday afternoon saying: 'And now it's over to Wimbledon for a bit of sphairistiké!' Fortunately for Des, and the sporting world in general, it was soon re-named lawn tennis.

Wingfield had introduced his new game during a Christmas party at a country house in Nantclywd, Wales, the previous year. Unlike the rectangular court at Leamington, Wingfield's court was shaped like an hour-glass, tapering at the net! A bust of Major Wingfield, bearing the inscription 'The Founder of Lawn Tennis' can be found in the offices of the Lawn Tennis Association.

Wingfield was, interestingly, a direct relation of John Wingfield, the English gaoler for Charles d'Orléans, a grandson of Charles VI of France, himself an enthusiastic tennis player.

Lawn tennis was seen as a game that could be played by both men and women, hence its rapid increase in popularity. But Wingfield's court and basic rules left a lot to be desired.

Later in 1874, the first game of lawn tennis ever to take place in the United States was played by Dr James Dwight and F.R. Sears.

The All-England Croquet Club had been founded in 1868, and two years later opened at its headquarters in Worple Road, Wimbledon. In 1875 the club agreed to set aside part of the ground for the playing of lawn tennis and badminton. Within a few months the first standardized set of lawn tennis rules had been drawn up, and by the end of that year the first American club was opened at Staten Island.

Over a short period, lawn tennis had rapidly grown in popularity as a leisure pursuit.

The All-England Croquet Club changed its name in 1877 to incorporate the words 'lawn tennis', and in 1882 the word croquet was dropped. It was reinstated in 1899 when the club assumed its present name, the All-England Lawn Tennis and Croquet Club.

In June 1877 the committee agreed to organize a championship to be called the Championships in Lawn Tennis, which was to herald the start of the most famous tennis event in the world – the Wimbledon Championships.

Between 9 and 19 July 1877 twenty-one players fought out the Championship, and the first winner was Spencer William Gore who beat William Marshall 6–1, 6–2, 6–4 in front of just 200 spectators. A far cry from the 15,000 that fill the Centre Court today!

The United States Lawn Tennis Association was founded in 1881 and later that year they organized their first Championships at Newport, Rhode Island. Men's singles and doubles were held.

The first women's singles at Wimbledon took place in 1884, while it was 1887 before they were introduced into the US Championships. Men's doubles also officially made its debut at Wimbledon in 1884, while the first official women's and mixed doubles were not held until 1913. The first French Championships were held in 1891 but were open only to members of French clubs and did not become an international event until 1925. The fourth leg of the Grand Slam, the Australian Championships, were inaugurated in 1905.

Tennis is currently making a comeback as an Olympic sport but it was included in the first modern Games at Athens in 1896 and at every celebration up until 1924.

Tennis had certainly spread internationally in its early years, and in 1883 the first match between the British Isles and United States took place at Wimbledon. The following year three Americans became the first of many to make an assault on the Wimbledon Championships. This international appeal led to the founding of the Davis Cup, the game's most important international team event. The United States easily beat the British Isles at Boston, Massachusetts in 1900 to win the first trophy. The winning captain was Dwight F. Davis, the man who presented the trophy.

To confirm the sport's appeal all over the world the International Lawn Tennis Federation was formed in March 1913. The majority of the twelve founder members were European, including Russia, but other founders included South Africa and Australasia.

A significant year in tennis history was 1922. In that year seeding was first introduced into the US Championships. (Two years later it was first used at Wimbledon.) But 1922 was also a special year in the All-England Club's history. Firstly, the club moved from Worple Road to its present home at Church Road. Secondly, the 1922 Championships were the first to be conducted on a knockout basis.

From the time of the inauguration of the Championships in 1877, they had been conducted on a challenge basis. In other words, the defending champion(s) had only to play one match to retain his or her title. The challenger was, however, found as the result of a knockout tournament. Consequently it meant that such men as William Renshaw, Reggie and Laurie Doherty and Tony Wilding were installed as champion and were difficult to remove. Renshaw held the title for six consecutive years.

The abolition of the challenge system heralded a succession of new names in the tennis world. Four Frenchmen dominated the game in both their own country and at Wimbledon in those early years – Jean Borotra, Henri Cochet, Rene Lacoste and Jacques Brugnon. Collectively they became known as 'The Four Musketeers'. Between them they won the men's singles at Wimbledon six times in the first eight years after the abolition of the challenge system. Their domination was broken in the late 1930s when Britain produced its own hero – Fred Perry, the last British men's singles champion at Wimbledon.

In 1938 the American Donald Budge became the first man to achieve the Grand Slam, the winning of the four major tournaments in one year – Wimbledon, the United States, France and Australia. Since then only one other man has performed the feat; Australia's Rod Laver, who won all four titles in both 1962 and 1969.

Women have also had their heroines over the years; Lottie Dod, the youngest ever Wimbledon champion at the age of fifteen, dominated the women's game in the early years. She was later to become an outstanding champion at golf as well. Suzanne Lenglen of France flew the flag for the fair sex while the Four Musketeers were dominating the men's game, but the inter-war years of women's tennis were dominated by Helen Wills-Moody of the United States, who won the women's title at Wimbledon a record-running eight times.

Overleaf: *Wimbledon champion Michael Stich prepares to play a forehand drive*

After the war, Maureen Connolly, affectionately known as 'Little Mo', became the first woman to perform the Grand Slam, in 1953. Margaret Court is the only other woman to have won all four titles in the same season, although Martina Navratilova has held all four major titles simultaneously, though without winning all four in the same year. Surprisingly Billie Jean King, winner of a record twenty Wimbledon titles, never performed the Grand Slam.

The big four Championships were strictly amateur events. Many top players, however, particularly in the 1950s and 1960s, left the amateur game to join the increasing number of professional tours that were being established. Rothmans then sponsored a tournament at Beckenham, Kent for professional tennis players, and it did not take long for the sport to develop into the big money-spinner it is today.

The sport went 'open' in 1968, when the British Hard Court Championships at Bournemouth staged tennis's first Open event. Later that year Rod Laver returned to Wimbledon as a professional and won his fourth title.

The tie-break, which eliminates lengthy sets, was first used in 1970 despite being in existence since 1926 when, amongst others, Suzanne Lenglen turned professional. Never again will Wimbledon see a scoreline like: 22–24, 1–6, 16–14, 6–3 11–9. That was the score in the men's singles when Pancho Gonzales beat Charlie Pasarell in 1969. In 1963 the first signs of commercialism and sponsorship of today's game had been seen and were introduced to the Wimbledon Championships the following year.

For a long time American and Australian players dominated both men's and women's tennis, but in the 1970s that began to change as the Europeans came to the fore.

The Davis Cup, which had, like the other big tournaments, been run on a challenge basis since its inception, became a knockout event in 1973. New nations such as Romania, Czecho-slovakia and Sweden emerged and became a threat to the 'big two'. Stars like Ilie Nastase, Bjorn Borg, Ivan Lendl and, more recently, West Germany's Boris Becker emerged to rival Jimmy Connors and John McEnroe of the United States.

Bjorn Borg's post-war record of winning the men's singles at Wimbledon five years in succession is unlikely to be beaten in the forseeable future. But in Martina Navratilova, women's tennis has

Borg's equal. In fact she can go one better: she has won the ladies' title six years in succession and eight times altogether.

At one time tennis was played only on grass, but it is now played on a variety of surfaces. There are the artificial surfaces, turf, hard courts (concrete or shale) and indoor surfaces such as wood or concrete covered by an artificial mat which resembles grass.

For nearly 100 years there has been little change in the size of the tennis court, height of net and size of ball. The current dimensions of the court (23.77m/78ft x 10.97m/36ft) were adopted in 1880, and two years later the net was standardized at a height of 0.91m (3ft) at the centre and 1.07m (3ft 6in) at the posts. The first court at the Leamington Club was 27.43m (90ft) x 10.97m (36ft) with a net 1.22m (4ft) high.

It was more than 100 years before any legislation was made about the racket, in terms of either its size or construction. In 1977, however, double stringing became popular, and the International Tennis Federation finally made a specific recommendation by immediately outlawing this innovation.

Tennis is an inexpensive sport to take up. You can buy a racket fairly cheaply (there again, you can also pay a small fortune for one!), and the cost of hiring a court at your local park or tennis centre is nominal, particularly if there are four of you playing. Most municipal parks have hard courts.

Tennis is taught in most schools, and these days the game can be played all the year round because of the development of indoor tennis centres and clubs. Tennis coaches are based throughout Britain, and if you contact the Lawn Tennis Association they will put you in touch with one in your area. Once you feel ready to go on and play a better standard of tennis, then you can join a local tennis club. Most clubs accept members at early ages, and for the betterment of the game players are encouraged to join a club as young as possible.

Equipment & terminology

Before we set about explaining the rules and telling you how to play tennis, you ought to familiarize yourself with the essential tennis equipment and get to know the court.

The court

As we said in the opening chapter, tennis is played on a variety of surfaces these days. Climates often dictate the use of certain surfaces, and worldwide a selection of courts constructed on grass, sand, clay, asphalt, cement and shale can be found. Indoor courts are usually cement or carpet. However, the majority of courts you will find yourself playing on will be hard courts, generally constructed of concrete, with a rubberized surface.

The court is rectangular and measures 23.77m (78ft) in length by 10.97m (36ft) wide. Within that area are two strips, one down each of the long sides of the court. These are 1.37m (4ft 6in) wide and known as the tramlines. They are used only in doubles play. In singles they have no use and any ball landing in the tramlines is out.

The court is divided into two halves by a net stretched across

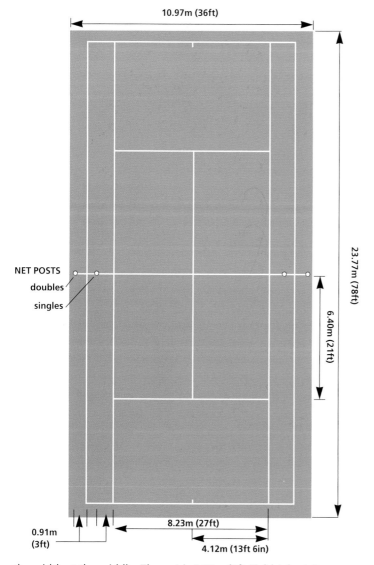

10.97m (36ft)

23.77m (78ft)

6.40m (21ft)

NET POSTS

doubles

singles

0.91m
(3ft)

8.23m (27ft)

4.12m (13ft 6in)

the width at the middle. The net is 1.07m (3ft 6in) high at the supporting posts and 0.91m (3ft) at the centre.

The lines determining the outer sides of the court are called
sidelines and those which determine the outer ends of the court are
known as baselines. In addition to these lines there are three other
markings in each half of the court.

A service line is marked parallel to the net and at a point 6.4m
(21ft) from the net. The service line does not extend into the

tramlines. Another line is then drawn from the centre of the net to the centre of the service line. Two boxes have now been created and when serving, the ball must land in either of these boxes, depending on which side the service is made from.

The final court marking is at the middle of the baseline. It is a small mark indicating the middle of the baseline. Hardly surprisingly this mark is called the centre mark.

All court markings should be the same colour but they can vary in size. The centre service line must be 5cm (2in) wide, as must the centre mark (which is, in effect, an extension of the centre service line). All other markings must be between 2.5–5cm (1–2in) except the baseline which can be up to 10cm (4in) wide.

Right, that's the court dealt with. But before we move on to the next section I think we ought to have a closer look at the net.

The two posts which support the net must be positioned 0.91m (3ft) outside the playing area. As there are two playing areas, one for singles and one for doubles, the supporting posts have therefore got a different position for each game. But both must be 0.91m (3ft) outside the court. Most major venues will have two different nets, one for singles play and one for doubles play. However, if only one net is used for both games then 'singles sticks' have to be used for the singles game. These are inserted in the ground 0.91m (3ft) from the sideline, and support the net at a height of 1.07m (3ft 6in).

THE NET

If the same net is used for doubles and singles play, 'singles sticks' should be put in place when the singles game is played. These are 1.07m (3ft 6in) high and are positioned 0.91m (3ft) outside the singles sidelines. The doubles posts are positioned 0.91m (3ft) outside the doubles sidelines

The net is supported by a cord or metal cable and covered by white tape. The net is adjustable and a handle at one of the posts is provided for this purpose. You will quite often see players testing the height of the net at the centre by standing one racket on end and putting the head of another on top of it at right-angles. This is by no means accurate but, in the absence of any other means of checking the height, is a useful substitute.

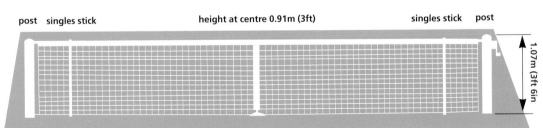

post   singles stick   height at centre 0.91m (3ft)   singles stick   post

1.07m (3ft 6in)

You have now learned what we are going to play the game on, but what are we going to play it with?

The racket

As we said earlier, for more than 100 years there was no legislation governing the tennis racket – either its size or what it was made of. But now there are certain limitations. The overall length of the frame, including the handle, must not exceed 81.28cm (32in) and the overall width should be no more than 31.75cm (12½in).

The racket frame is usually made of graphite and the head is generally strung with an artificial material like nylon although it may be a fibre-type string or even natural gut. The rules say that the hitting area must be flat and consist of a pattern of crossed strings connected to the frame. The stringing must be as uniform as possible and have the same density all over. The strung surface shall not exceed 39.3cm (15½in) in overall length or be greater than 29.21cm (11½in) wide.

Rackets vary in weight according to personal preference, but the average is 368.55–396.90g (12–14oz).

The ball

The tennis ball is made of rubber and covered with wool or any acceptable man-made substitute, but it must not have stitched

THE RACKET
The modern graphite rackets

THE BALL

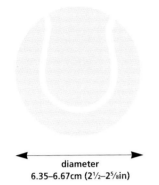

diameter
6.35–6.67cm (2½–2⅝in)

seams. When made, each ball should be pressurized so that when dropped on to a concrete surface from a height of 2.54m (100in) it will bounce to 1.35–1.47m (53–58in). The diameter of the ball is 6.35–6.67cm (2½–2⅝in) and weight 56.70–58.50g (2–2¹⁄₁₆oz). White balls are now uncommon as yellow has become the popular and accepted colour.

In major tournament play balls are kept refrigerated. Normally six balls are in play at any one time, and because they change pressure and shape through being constantly hit, the balls are changed at the end of the first seven games, and every nine thereafter.

Finally, clothing. As in all sports it is important to feel comfortable when playing tennis. Your feet need particular attention because they take some hammering during a game which, if it goes to five sets, can take a good three or four hours to complete.

Tennis shoes

A wide selection of tennis shoes (affectionately called 'trainers') are available in most shoe shops and sports goods shops. The prices vary from £30 to well over £150. Naturally, the funds available help you in making such a choice, but often shoes in the £40–50 range are as acceptable as those at the top end of the market.

These days they are made from very lightweight materials which put less strain on the feet. Believe me, at the end of three or four hours of tennis the feet and legs wish they were soaking in a nice warm bath rather than running round after a little yellow ball on a tennis court! Make sure any shoes you buy are ventilated.

Clothing

Again, tennis clothing comes in a wide range of prices. The important thing about clothing is to feel comfortable and have the

TENNIS SHOES
It is important that your shoes should be:
(a) comfortable
(b) lightweight and
(c) ventilated

freedom to move easily.

White was the traditional colour of tennis players' clothing for over 100 years, but the trend is to wear coloured clothing covered in patterns and motifs, although Wimbledon still insists on a white base for shirts and shorts (or skirts).

Men wear shorts with pockets in which to put a spare ball when not in use, while women wear skirts, although some wear shorts. Skirts can also come with an internal pocket in which to house a ball.

The right choice of socks is important. You would be silly to wear a nylon pair to play tennis in. White cotton ones are far more practical.

If you perspire a lot, sweat bands, both for the wrist and head, are worth investing in. There is nothing worse than having a stream of sweat constantly rolling down your forehead and into your eyes.

You are well advised to take a towel on to court with you and a bottle of something cool to drink (but not fizzy) is also a good idea.

That's it. You now know what you are going to play on, you know what you are going to play with, and you know how to dress properly and sensibly. It's nearly time to learn how to play the game! But first of all, let's look at some tennis terms you will come across during the rest of the book and when you are playing and watching the game. Understanding the terms used in tennis is just as important as understanding the rules.

CLOTHING
This is how you should dress for a game of tennis

TERMINOLOGY

Ace A serve which the receiver cannot get to and return is an ace. If he or she gets their racket to the ball but fails to return it, then it is NOT an ace, but just a good winning serve.

Advantage If the score goes to deuce (see scoring on page 34) the next point won is known as advantage, and to the person who won the point.

Approach shot A shot made before taking up a position at the net.

Backhand A shot played with the reverse side of the racket and with the back of the hand facing the ball.

THE BACKHAND

Ball boy (or girl) In major championships, ball boys (or girls) are employed to collect stray balls in between rallies so as not to interrupt the players' concentration. When playing at your local park, however, you do not have that luxury and have to take it in turns to go out of the court to find balls hit over the surrounding fence.

Ball in play The ball is in play from the moment it is hit in the service. Unless a fault or let is called it remains in play until the point is decided.

Baseline The line marking the end of the court is the baseline.

Baseline play When play takes place with the players hitting the ball to each other from near the baseline.

Centre line The name given to the line that divides the service court into two halves. If the server is delivering to the service court on his left, he must stand to the right of the centre line, and vice versa. The receiver may stand wherever he sees fit, so long as he remains on his side of the net!

Centre service line The real, more specific name for the centre line.

Cross-court drive A shot played diagonally across the court.

Deep volley A volley that lands close to your opponent's baseline.

Deuce If each player wins three points then the score becomes deuce. The next point becomes 'advantage' to one player (see page 22). If the scores become level after the next rally, it returns to deuce, and so on.

Double fault If you fail to make a proper serve with your two attempts it is a double fault and your opponent wins the point.

Doubles A match involving two players per side. They can be two players either of the same sex (men's or women's doubles) or of the opposite sex (mixed doubles).

Drop shot A shot played so that it drops just over the net. It is normally played with backspin to prevent it bouncing too high once it goes over the net.

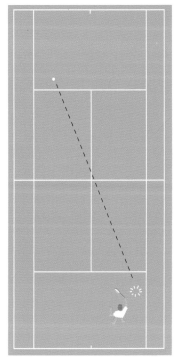

THE CROSS-COURT DRIVE
A shot played from one side of the court to the other is a cross-court drive

Fault A serve that either goes into the net or does not first land in the correct service court is a fault. If the next serve is also a fault then it is a double fault and the server loses the point.

Flat service A service made by striking the ball with a flat racket face and thus not applying spin to the ball.

THE DROP SHOT
A ball delicately played so that it falls to the ground just beyond the net is known as a drop shot

Playing a forehand

Foot fault A service that infringes the foot-fault rules (see page 32) is a foot fault and is treated like an ordinary fault.

Forehand A shot made with the front face of the racket and with the forearm facing the ball is a forehand shot.

Game A game lasts until one player has won four points, provided he has won at least two more than his opponent. If not, the game continues until he is two points clear, at which stage he wins the game.

Ground stroke A shot played after the ball has bounced.

Half-volley A stroke made at the same moment as the ball hits the ground is a half-volley.

In A ball is said to be 'in' if any part of it lands within the confines of the court.

Let As in most racket sports, in tennis the let is used to replay a point. If a player is interfered with by an outside source or a serve is made before the receiver is ready, then a let is called. However, in tennis the let also has another meaning.

If the service hits the net cord and bounces into the correct service court, the point is replayed without penalty. However, if it hits the net and bounces OUT of the service court or into the wrong service court then it is a fault. In major championships, a net cord judge sits at the net post to make a decision on whether it is a let or not, although this job is increasingly done electronically.

Linesmen (or women) At major events linesmen (or women) assist the umpire in deciding whether a ball is in or out of court. The umpire can overrule a linesman's call if he thinks he (she) made the wrong call.

Lob A shot directed high into the air and into your opponent's half of the court.

Love If a player has not scored a point his score is 'love'.

Love game A game in which one player wins without his opponent scoring a point.

Match A match consists of a pre-determined number of sets. Normally five in men's singles and men's doubles, and three for women's singles and doubles, and mixed doubles.

SET	1	2	3	4	5
J. SMITH	6	6	6	1	8
A. BROWN	4	3	7	6	10

SCORING
This is how the scores might look at the end of a five-set match. Brown won by three sets to two – having been two sets down!

Match point If a player needs just one point to win the match he is said to have match point. If he leads 40–30 he has one match point. If the score is 40–15 he has two match points and if it is 40–love then he has three match points.

Net game When a player adopts a position close to the net and begins a volleying game he is said to be playing a 'net game'.

New balls As we said earlier, new balls are normally introduced into major championships every nine games. It is up to the player serving with the new balls to indicate to the receiver, normally by holding the balls up, to show they are new.

Out A ball is 'out' if no part of it lands within the confines of the court.

Passing shot A shot which goes past your opponent while he or she is at the net is a passing shot.

Rally A sequence of shots made by the players to each other is a rally.

Referee The supreme official at any event or championship. He or she is responsible for the overall control of the event and has the power to overrule the umpire's decisions.

THE PASSING SHOT
A winning passing shot

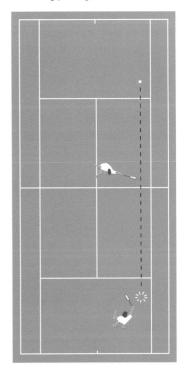

Seeding Lawn tennis has had seeding for more than sixty years. The idea of seeding is to make sure the best players remain in the competition as long as possible. Theoretically the number one and two seeds should contest every final, while the three and four seeds should make it to the semi-final stage, and so on. Happily, outsiders frequently come along and upset the seedings, otherwise tennis would be pretty boring.

Service The stroke that starts each point. The service must be made by hitting the ball into the opposite service court and it must bounce before being returned.

Set A set consists of at least six games. The first person to win six games wins the set provided he is at least two games clear of his opponent. If not, the set continues until one player has the two-game advantage. If the tie-break is being used it comes into operation when the game gets to 6–all. Whoever wins the tie-break wins the set 7–6.

Set point Same as match point, except this time it is when one player is on the verge of winning the set.

Singles sticks If a court is fitted with one net for use in both singles and doubles matches a singles stick is placed in the ground 0.91m (3ft) from the sideline for a game of singles. It should support the net at a height of 1.07m (3ft 6in). The area of net between the singles stick and outer post is deemed to be a permanent fixture.

Slice A shot played with backspin and possibly sidespin.

Smash A ball hit above the head and powerfully into the opposing half of the court.

Stop volley A volley, usually made close to the net, which forces the ball to drop into your opponent's half of the court and just over the net.

Tie-break To prevent long sets the tie-break was introduced in 1970. If the number of games gets to 6–all then the tie-break is

Todd Martin in action at Wimbledon in 1996

played. The first person to reach seven points, provided he is at least two points clear of his opponent, wins the tie-break and the set. The tie-break may not be used in the final set of a match.

Topspin A deceptive shot with a lot of spin that causes the ball to dip sharply in flight.

Umpire Unfortunately, when you play at your local park you will not have the luxury of an umpire. The honesty and integrity of the two players will be called upon to decide dubious decisions. (If you are ever in any doubt, simply play a let.) However, in major championships the umpire sits on an elevated chair overlooking the net. He has control of play on the court and is responsible for keeping and confirming the score to the players.

Volley A stroke made before the ball hits the ground. The receiver can volley at any time except from the service, when he must let the serve bounce in the service court first.

UMPIRING
The umpire sits in an elevated chair positioned level with the net. He has a clear view of all the play

THE VOLLEY
To play a volley, you must strike the ball before it hits the ground

The brilliant Martina Hingis using her double-handed backhand to great effect

The game – a guide

As with other racket sports, the object of tennis is to win rallies in order to score points. However, unlike some similar sports you do not have to be the server to win points in lawn tennis. You can win points as either the server or receiver.

The object of the game is simple: to hit the ball over the net and into your opponent's half of the court so that he is unable to return it over the net to you.

A match consists of a pre-determined number of sets up to a maximum of five for a match involving men and three involving women.

The tossing of a coin or a racket shall decide which player serves first. Both players are entitled to a warm-up, or practice, period at the commencement of a match, or re-start of an interrupted match. Whoever wins the toss can choose whether he becomes the first server or receiver, in which case the other player has the choice of ends.

Alternatively, the player winning the toss can have the choice of ends, thus giving the other player the choice of serving or receiving. The players stand on opposite sides of the net.

THE SERVICE

Once the server has been established the first service starts the game. At the start of every new game the first service is always made from the server's right-hand side of the court and the ball must be hit over the net into the diagonally opposite service court. At the time of making the service the server must stand with both feet behind the baseline and between the imaginary extensions of the centre mark and sideline (not the extreme sideline, but the one indicating the extent of the singles court).

To make a legal and successful serve, the ball should be thrown into the air with the hand NOT holding the racket and, before it hits the ground, be hit by the racket. The service is deemed to be made the moment the racket makes contact with the ball. For the service to be good it must land in the diagonally opposite service court. If it does not, a fault is called and the server has a second chance to make a good serve. If that second serve

THE SERVICE
If you are serving from the right-hand court your feet must be placed within the shaded area. (Vice versa from the left-hand court)

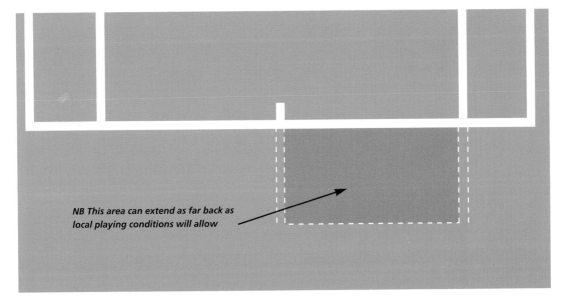

NB This area can extend as far back as local playing conditions will allow

should also be a fault then a double fault is called, and a point is awarded to the opposing player. The next point starts with the server standing on the opposite side of the baseline (i.e. to the left of the centre mark). Thereafter the service alternates from one side of the centre mark to the other in strict rotation, after every point has been played.

If, after a serve, the ball is returned by the receiver, then the rally continues until one player fails to return the ball or the ball is played into the net or out of the court. Once the rally is over, the next serve takes place and, as already said, from the opposite side of the centre mark.

FOOT FAULT
It is a foot fault if any part of the foot touches the baseline at the moment the racket makes contact with the ball

Foot fault

A server will be foot faulted if either foot touches any area other than that behind the baseline and within the imaginary extension of the centre mark and sideline. However, it is also a foot fault if a server changes his position by walking or running into the serve. A foot fault is treated like a normal fault.

Changing ends

Players change ends at the completion of the first, third and subsequent alternate games in each set. If the set ends on an odd number, say 6–3, the players change ends. They next change ends after the first game of the next set. However, if the set ends 6–4 then they do not change at the end of the set. They do, however, change after the first game of the following set. A rest period lasting a maximum ninety seconds is allowed while players are changing ends.

WINNING & LOSING POINTS

There are several ways in which points can be won or lost. The following are the most common ways.

At the service, the server wins the point if the ball hits the receiver, or any part of his clothing or his racket, before it hits the ground. If the receiver is unable to return the ball over the net after it has landed in the correct service court the server is awarded the point.

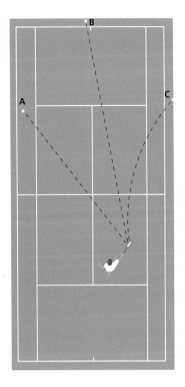

BALL HIT OUT
*The shots illustrated here (A, B, C)
are all 'out'. However, A would
be 'in' if you were playing
doubles*

The receiver automatically wins the point if the server double faults. At other times you will lose points if:

(a) You allow the ball in play to bounce twice before success-fully returning it over the net.

(b) You return a ball and it does not cross the net.

(c) You return a ball over the net but it bounces outside your opponent's half of the court. The ball is then said to be 'out'.

(d) You hit the ball more than once in one stroke.

(e) You volley the ball before it crosses the net.

(f) You, or anything you wear, or your racket, touches the net, net cord, net supporting posts or ground within your opponent's part of the court.

(g) You throw your racket at the ball … if you throw it at anything, or anybody else, you can expect an even more severe penalty!

(h) The ball comes into contact with you or any of your clothing, other than your racket.

VOLLEYING ON THE WRONG SIDE OF THE NET
You are not allowed to volley the ball until it has crossed the net into your half of the court

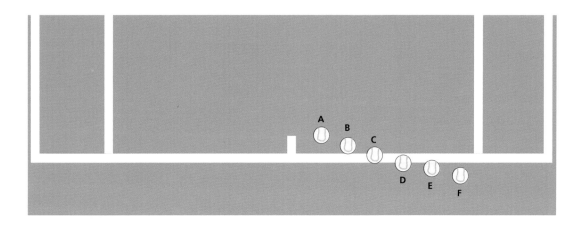

BALL IN OR OUT OF COURT
The ball must be wholly over the line
to be out. In this diagram only ball F is
out. Now do you see what a difficult
job line judges have?

Umpires these days are concerned about the increasing amount of misconduct on court and they have the power to award conduct violation points against a player for any action that they feel is not within the spirit of the game. Persistently breaking the rules can cost you the match. You have been warned.

In addition to the above, you will also lose the point if it is deemed that you have deliberately hindered your opponent in making a stroke.

Ball in or out

A ball is deemed to be in the court if any part of it hits the sideline or baseline. The same applies if the ball hits the service or centre service line at the service.

Now for the important part …

SCORING

Scoring in tennis is simple, not that you would think so when you listen to some players!

The first point won by a player is called 15; the second is 30; and the third 40. The next point is game. A player can only win a game when he is two points clear of his opponent. So, if the score gets to 40–30, the player on 40 will win the game if he wins the next point. However, if he loses the next point the score goes to 'deuce' and the game continues until one player has a two-point advantage.

To clarify the scoring even further, let us assume two players (A and B) are taking part in a singles match. This is how the scoring would go:

Point won by	Score A	B
A	15	love
A	30	love
B	30	15
A	40	15
B	40	30
B	Deuce	
A	Advantage A	
B	Deuce	
B	Advantage B	
B	Game B	

After Advantage A, Player A lost the next point so the score reverted to deuce. Player B then won two successive points and so took the game. What could be simpler?

The set scoring has already been outlined in the Terminology section on page 26.

Tie-break

Most competitions use the tie-break, and the major championships have been using it since the early 1970s.

Numerical scoring (1, 2, 3, etc.) – as opposed to conventional tennis scoring (15, 30, 40) – is used throughout the tie-break. The person who should be serving next, if the match was continuing normally, serves first in the tie-break. He serves only for the first point, after which the service passes to the other player, who serves for two points. The players then take it in turns to serve for two points alternately until a winner has been found.

The first player to reach seven points wins the tie-break. However, like most aspects of tennis, you have to be two points clear of your opponent before you win the tie-break. You cannot win it 7–6, 8–7, 9–8 etc. It must be 7–5, 8–6, 9–7 and so on. As the tie-break is a game, the set score will be 7–6, with the tie-break score usually put in brackets afterwards.

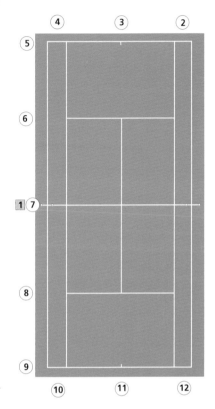

JUDGES' POSITIONS
If the umpire receives the assistance of judges, this is where they sit. All major championship matches are adjudicated by this many officials. Some top tournaments use an 'electronic eye' on the service line to help with decisions about the service
1 = umpire
6 and 8 = service line judges
3 and 11 = centre service line judges
7 = net cord judge
All other judges rule whether balls are in or out, and assist with foot fault decisions

THE OFFICIALS

In practice the majority of matches are played without any official. It is up to the players to be honest with each other (and themselves) and make decisions that will affect the game. However, at club level, an umpire will officiate over any match which is a league game or similar. At international and major championship level the umpire will be assisted by judges.

Unless a referee is appointed, the umpire is the sole arbitrator. However, if there is a referee, appeals can be made to him, and he has the power to overrule any decisions made by the umpire.

If an umpire receives assistance from judges they will be positioned as shown in the diagram and their task is to make decisions on points of fact i.e. if a ball was in or out, or whether the service was a foot fault, or whether the ball was a let. If judges are not in a position to make such a decision they should indicate accordingly to the umpire who should take on the task himself. If he cannot make a decision, he has the power to call a let.

DOUBLES PLAY

The first thing to remember about doubles play is that the court area is larger by virtue of the fact that the tramlines come into play making the playing area 9ft (2.74m) wider.

The service is the same in doubles play as in singles and must be made to the diagonal service box. However, the order of service must be decided at the beginning of each set and adhered to throughout that set.

If you serve in game 1 then your partner will serve in game 3. Game 2 is served by one of your opponents while game 4 is served by the other member of the opposing side. That order must be retained throughout the set. It can be changed at the commencement of the next set.

The team who are the receivers in the first game decides which player shall receive the first service. That player then receives the first service in every odd-numbered game throughout the set. The other team, when they become receivers, make the same

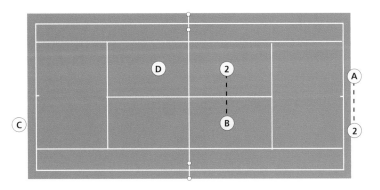

SERVING IN DOUBLES
A and B are playing together, and C and D form the other pair. In the first game, A serves to C for the first service. At the start of the second point he serves to D, but from position 2. B also moves to his position 2. At the end of the game C serves next to either A or B, then in the third game B serves, starting with C. Finally, in the fourth service game, D serves to either A or B, who shall be the same player who first received the service from C at the beginning of the match. And so it continues, in the same order

choice, and that player receives the first service in every even-numbered game throughout the set.

The server will, as in singles, start the game by serving from the right-hand side of the court, and alternately after each point. The receiving players do not change sides after each point, they retain their positions and take it in turn to become a receiver.

Once the serve has been returned the rally continues and either player from one side can play the ball; they do not have to play alternate shots as in table tennis.

If a service hits the server's partner then it is a fault. If it hits the receiver's partner before the ball hits the ground the serving team win the point.

If the tie-break is introduced into a doubles game then the player who is scheduled to serve next serves the first point. There-after the service alternates as in the singles game but in accordance with the order already played within the set. The pair who serve first in the tie-break game will receive the first service in the opening game of the next set.

Overleaf: David Prinosil serves during the German Open at Hamburg in 1996

Rules
clinic

As a player it is important to know and understand all the rules of tennis so that you feel confident, especially when a new situation arises in a match.

What happens if a service is made from the wrong half of the court?
All play resulting from the service will stand, but the moment the error is spotted the correct serving point should be taken up before the next service.

If I notice my opponent served from the wrong half of the court on his first service and it was a fault, does he have to complete the service from that half of the court or should he move to the correct half immediately?
He should move to the correct half of the court immediately, but has only one service left on that point.

If my opponent serves and then I realize it is my turn to serve what happens?
The fault should be rectified immediately, but all points scored before the error was noticed shall count. However, if the error is

noted after your opponent has served a fault, the fault does not carry over to you when you become the server.

What about doubles? Surely it must happen often that the wrong player serves? What happens then?
Well, it doesn't happen at the top level, but it does happen in the local park or tennis centre. Once the error is discovered the correct sequence should be reverted to and all points scored during the error shall count. The same applies if the receivers take the service in the wrong order.

If players go to the wrong ends after changing service when should the error be rectified?
As soon as it is noticed. All points scored up to that time shall count however.

During an indoor game, the ball from a service hits a rafter and then bounces into the correct service court. Is the service good or not?
It would be a fault. Any ball that hits a permanent fixture from the service is a fault. Permanent fixtures include such things as stands, permanent seating and their occupants … which could well be a judge!

If the server throws the ball up and then fails to hit it, is it a fault?
Yes. Just like in golf, it is a 'fresh air' shot, and counts.

… but if the server decides to abort the serve after throwing the ball up, is it still a fault?
No.

Is a let called if the ball hits the top of the net and goes into the correct court during a normal rally?
No. It can only be called a let at the service.

Can I catch the ball on my racket?
Yes, you most probably can. But if you do the point goes to your opponent!

Overleaf: Tim Henman thrills the Wimbledon crowd with his flair and determination

If you throw the ball up to serve, swing at it and miss, it is a fault

What happens if a ball becomes damaged during a rally?
A let should be called and the point should be replayed.

If I play a shot then deliberately hit my racket on to the ground and distort the shape of it before returning the ball for a winning shot do I still get the point?
No. You are not allowed to deliberately and materially change the shape of your racket during the playing of a point. Mind you, if you have time to damage your racket, and then play a winning shot you must be some player ...

What happens if my racket becomes damaged during a rally?
You will have to wait until the end of the point to change it.

If I play a shot that hits the ground within the confines of the court and then hits the stop-netting at the back of the court before my opponent can reach it, is it a winning point?
Yes. The same applies if the ball hits any other permanent fixture,

provided you hit a good ball into the opposing court first.

If I return a ball and it hits the net post and then goes into the opposing court, does it count or is a let called?
It counts as a legitimate point.

You said earlier that I cannot lean over the net to volley a ball in the other half of the court. But what would happen if my opponent played a shot, it bounced in my half of the court and then the wind took it back again over to his side of the net?
You would be allowed to play the ball provided you did not touch the net with your body, clothing or racket.

What happens if my racket accidentally slips out of my hand and hits the net, do I lose the point?
Yes, provided the ball is in play at the time. Mind you, you were warned to take some talcum powder on to the court with you weren't you ...?

Does a player have to be standing in the court to make a shot?
No. He can be anywhere, except in his opponent's area of the court.

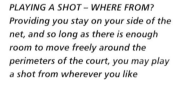

PLAYING A SHOT – WHERE FROM?
Providing you stay on your side of the net, and so long as there is enough room to move freely around the perimeters of the court, you may play a shot from wherever you like

If I play a volley close to the net, hit the ball in my half of the court, but then allow my racket to follow-through and go over the net, am I penalized?
No, but again you must make sure you don't touch the net.

Does a ball that hits another ball lying on the court have to be played as a let?
No, the shot counts. Mind you, if it happened at Wimbledon the umpire would certainly have a few choice words to say to the ball boy (or girl)!

If I am hindered from playing my shot is a let called?
Yes, unless you are hindered by a permanent fixture. Let's say a pigeon flies across your sight just as you're about to play, that is certainly outside interference, and a pigeon could not be described as a permanent fixture.

You keep mentioning 'permanent fixtures' … what exactly are they?
The laws of the game describe a permanent fixture thus: 'The net, posts, singles sticks, cord or metal cables, strap and band. Also, where there are any, the back and side stops, the stands, fixed or movable seats and chairs around the court, and their occupants, all other fixtures above and around the court, and the umpire, net-cord judge, foot-fault judge, linesmen and ball boys (or girls) when in their respective places.'

Where does the receiver have to stand when taking the service?
Anywhere, provided it is in his own half of the court. Understand-ably, it makes sense to stand in the half of the court to where the server is serving otherwise the job of returning the ball is consider-ably harder. How close you stand to the net depends on the strength of your opponent's serve.

How is the 1½ minute break in between games timed?
The time is taken from the moment the ball goes out of play at the end of the game to the time the ball is struck for the first point of the next game.

Is there a time limit on the amount of time a server can take in between the end of one point and serving to start the next?
In major international events this is normally 30 seconds.

How often are the balls changed during the tie-break game?
Not at all. The tie-break game is counted as one game for the purpose of the ball change. If the balls, however, are due to be changed at the beginning of the tie-break, the change is delayed until it is completed.

Can the server's feet be off the ground at the time of the service?
Yes, but at the moment of striking the ball his foot (or feet) must not touch the baseline or court the other side of the baseline.

Overleaf: *Emilio Alvarez of Spain whips a powerful backhand across court*

Technique

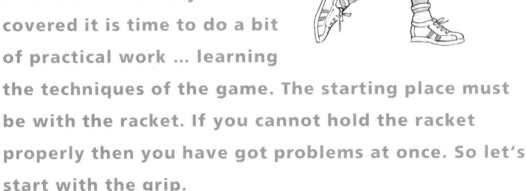

Now that the theory has been covered it is time to do a bit of practical work ... learning the techniques of the game. The starting place must be with the racket. If you cannot hold the racket properly then you have got problems at once. So let's start with the grip.

THE GRIP

It is important to realize that you need to adopt a different grip when playing different strokes.

    The most common grip, and the one used for the forehand drive, which will cater for the majority of your shots, is the semi-western forehand, whereby the thumb is moved back and the arm is slightly bent.

    Another grip is the western forehand, which is useful for those balls which bounce that bit higher. The thumb is moved

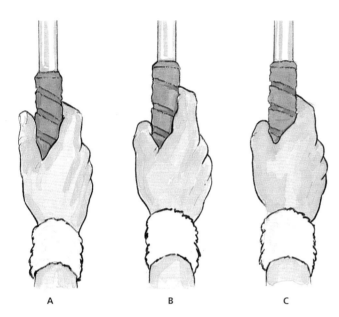

A   B   C

clockwise on to the top of the handle. Because the palm of the hand is 'under' the handle, it makes the playing of low shots that bit more difficult, but it is ideal for shots waist-high and above.

The eastern forehand is also known as the 'shake hands' grip because you grip the handle as if you were shaking hands with it. To make sure you adopt this grip correctly hold the racket in your left hand; place the palm of your right hand on the strings and slide it down the racket, keeping the palm in the same position, until you reach the handle. Now wrap your fingers around the handle ... shake hands with it if you like. You should now have complete control of the racket for playing those forehand shots.

The next grip we will look at is for the backhand drive.

Many inexperienced players have a difficult time playing the backhand. But this inability to play the shot – or should we call it fear – stems from the fact that a poor grip is adopted. The main cause of this is the difficulty most novices have in changing their grip to the backhand during a rally. But remember, you will have extreme difficulty playing a successful backhand shot unless you change your grip.

To change your grip into a backhand grip you should move your hand anti-clockwise around the handle so that your thumb

THE FOREHAND GRIP (A)
The semi-western is the most common forehand grip

THE BACKHAND GRIP (B)
Note how the hand is moved anti-clockwise around the handle and the thumb is tucked under the handle for extra support

THE CHOPPER (SERVICE) GRIP (C)
Make sure your fingers are not too close together. Note the first finger – doesn't it look as though it is going to pull the trigger of a gun?

nicely tucks underneath and the palm of your hand is now more on top of the handle. The effect of wrapping the thumb around the handle is to put the firmness into the grip and stroke.

It is important to make sure the fingers are not too close together again, otherwise the grip will be too wristy. It is also essential with the backhand shot to make sure the wrist is locked solid on to the handle.

A common fault with novices when playing the backhand is to play the shot with slice i.e. the racket slides under the ball and imparts spin. The racket head should be played through the ball with an open face. There are times when you will want to play the backhand with slice, but that is a specialist shot, and not one that you should be playing just yet.

Many players adopt the two-handed grip for the backhand. The same grip as above is adopted but the other hand is placed adjacent to the gripping hand to give extra support and power.

The biggest problem you will encounter initially is the ability to change grips fast enough during an actual rally. But don't worry, it will come in time and you will soon be able to change without thinking about it. Simply because you lack the confidence to play the backhand, don't rely on the forehand for all your shots.

I cannot stress enough at this stage that you should practise the backhand shot. There is no sense in being good at the forehand without being able to introduce other shots into your repertoire.

There are more grips you need to learn. For serving and playing the overhead smash you are well advised to adopt the 'chopper' or continental grip. The serve is like a throw and the chopper grip makes the action easier.

For playing the forehand or backhand volley you should adopt the same grips as for the eastern forehand and backhand drives or a continental grip for both volleys. This grip will enable you, after serving, to progress to the net to play a volley without having to change your grip. But we will look at all that a little bit later.

Finally, whereabouts should you grip the handle? Answer: as near as possible to the end. That way you will get the maximum effect of the racket. If you have to grip the handle nearer to the head because it is too heavy then you are well advised to get a lighter racket.

There are five fundamentals you should always bear in mind: (1) watch the ball; (2) have good balance and footwork; (3) make sure you have a good swing on the ground strokes, a punch action on the volley and a throwing action on the serve; (4) control the racket movement; and (5) control the racket face.

You should always watch the ball. You must keep your eye on that ball as it leaves your opponent right up to the moment it makes contact with your racket. Get into the habit of doing that right from the start. If you don't you will find that a lot of your shots are rushed.

TWO-HANDED BACKHAND
Note how the normally redundant left hand adds support and power to the racket as this right-handed player plays a backhand

Getting quickly around the court is important, but it is no use getting into the right position if you are off balance. Think what you are doing with your feet all the time, because good footwork helps create good balance. Recover quickly after you have hit the ball so that you are ready for the next shot.

Having got into a balanced position, you should have no problem in hitting the ball on the ground strokes. Both the backswing and follow-through should be fluent. Provided your balance and footwork are right then you should have little diffi-culty in perfecting a good swing.

However, if there are some flaws in your footwork then control-ling the racket movement is going to prove difficult. You must have complete control over the racket. Don't expect it to do all the work. It is like a computer, it will only do what the operator tells it to!

Controlling the racket face is as important as any of the other fundamentals, because if you cannot control the face then you are not likely to play any winning shots. Racket face control comes down to the right grip for the right shot. Keep the grip firm and imagine the racket as an extension to your arm.

PLAYING THE DIFFERENT SHOTS

Right, you know how to hold the racket for the different shots. It is time we taught you how to play the shots.

The shot that starts off each point is the Service. If you watch the top players you will be astounded at the pace they put into the service stroke, and with consistent accuracy. However, whatever you do, don't try and emulate the likes of Pete Sampras, Greg Rusedski or Goran Ivanisevic the first time you try to serve. Don't run before you can walk. Experience will tell you when you are ready to start experimenting with a more powerful serve and one with spin. However, we will look at the basics. Incidentally, the following assumes that you are right-handed.

THE SERVICE
Left foot pointing towards net post, racket pointing towards service court ...

... 'Place' the ball up ...

... Ball going up, racket going back ...

You take up position with a sideways stance. Your left foot should point towards the right-hand net post. The feet should be 38–45cm (15–18in) apart. The racket head should be pointing towards the service court you intend serving to. Your two hands should be in contact with the racket but as you drop your racket ready to go into the backswing, your left hand (the one holding the ball) swings into an upright position. It then releases the ball upwards. Many novices make the mistake of releasing the ball too early and it is thrown at an angle and towards the net rather than upwards – consequently you have to stretch to play the shot. The correct position of the ball at the moment of impact should be in front of the left foot. The ball should be thrown to a height just above your normal reach.

... and contact the ball at top of reach ...

... Eye on ball ... begin to throw the racket up ...

... Finally, the follow-through

While the ball is on its way upwards, the racket should start its 'throwing' movement into the ball. Your bodyweight is now starting to switch from your back foot to your front foot. At the top of the reach the racket arm should be perfectly straight and you should reach as far as possible to hit the ball. The head of the racket should be 'thrown' in an 'up-and-over' action and should hit the falling ball accurately. If you don't keep your eyes on the ball there is little chance of you making a good service.

After making contact with the ball you should follow through, and the momentum of the swing will carry you forward and into the court ready to meet any return. Some players like to get close to the net as soon as possible after making the service but, like all aspects of the game, that comes with confidence and experience.

The most common error in serving is in the placing of the ball. You will at first find a lack of consistency in this respect. You are well advised in your early days of development to concentrate on getting the placement right and just making sure the ball goes into the correct service court. At this stage, the service will have little impact on the outcome of the game, so just concentrate on developing a simple but effective service. Getting the co-ordination between left and right hand is more important than anything. Once you have that sorted out then serving will become second nature. When you are ready, try to develop a second serve applied with spin.

Once you have mastered the serve you need to experiment by trying to place the ball into one half or the other of the service court, thus confusing your opponent. If you know he is weak on his backhand, then you should regularly serve to his backhand.

That's the service out of the way. But what happens if your opponent returns it … you have got to know what shot to play, and how to play it.

The forehand drive

The forehand drive is the most widely used shot in a game of tennis. It is also the easiest to play. Because of this, many inexperienced players rely on the shot too much and rather than adopt a position to play the backhand will get in position, albeit the wrong one, to play the forehand. However, you will use it a lot, so let's see how to play it.

THE FOREHAND DRIVE
Far left: *The 'ready' position*
Left: *Feet nicely in position, knees slightly bent*

Right: *Shot played with the contact point slightly in front, but not too close to the body*
Far right: *The follow-through*

Total concentration is shown by Michael Chang – one of the many qualitites that has made him one of the most consistent players of recent years

Once you can see the ball is coming to your forehand make sure you have the correct grip (you won't have time to look at your grip, but you will be able to tell by the feel). When you play the forehand shot, the ball will be to your right so you have to make sure your feet are in the correct position. If you leave it too late to get into position you will be in awful trouble and will have to play the ball hurriedly and too close to your body. The result will be either a losing shot or a poor return.

I know you will not have a lot of time to get everything right, and it will take many hours of practice before these steps become instinctive. But you need to have your weight forward on the balls of your feet at the 'ready' position. The racket head should be approximately waist-high and the left hand should support the racket just below the head.

As you begin to play the shot the body will turn away from the ball. The wrist should be kept firm, and as you take the racket into the backswing the left arm can be outstretched to help with your balance. As the shot is made, your body will turn towards the ball. The racket should make contact with the ball at a comfortable distance and should be rising as it hits the ball. Again, keep your eyes on the ball up to the point of impact – this cannot be stressed enough. After completing the shot the racket should follow through and you should quickly get into position for your next shot … unless you have played a winning shot of course!

Of course, playing deceptive shots is all part of the game, and the forehand lends itself to greater scope in the playing of such shots. The forehand shot can be hit with topspin, underspin or flat (with no spin at all). Of course, how you hit the ball determines where it is going to land on the other side of the net. You have to quickly assess your opponent's position and decide whether you are going to play a powerful passing drive or a cross-court shot. Only a specific game situation will dictate this decision.

The backhand drive

This shot petrifies new players but if you can get it into your head that it is just as easy to play as the forehand then you should have no problems.

As you move into position, your weight goes on to the back foot and the turning of the body into a sideways position starts on that foot. The racket head is again held approximately waist-high, and is once more supported by the left hand.

When the racket moves into the backswing position, all your body weight is on the back foot and your right foot steps forward ready for you to play the ball from a sideways hitting position. The shot is played with a lot of movement of the shoulders, which rotate 90 degrees into the shot. At the same time the weight is transferred to the front foot. The shot is made with the ball a comfortable distance away and in an upward motion.

The most important thing to remember when playing the backhand drive is keep that wrist firm. If you don't, you will just 'kill' the ball when it hits the racket and the ball will most probably end up in the net …

When playing the double-handed backhand, grip the racket with the left hand above the right. Both hands should hold the racquet firmly. Footwork is the same as in the single-handed backhand but you might find that your balance is slightly more difficult to control. You may need to take an extra step with your back foot after making the shot.

THE BACKHAND DRIVE
Left to right: Keep your eye on the ball as it approaches, and move into position. Move your weight on to your back foot. Now step forward with the right, and transfer your weight to that foot. Play the shot with a firm wrist and keep the face of the racket 'open'. Finally, don't forget that flowing follow-through!

The double-handed backhand gives you more power and control, but you have to move well to get in position to make the

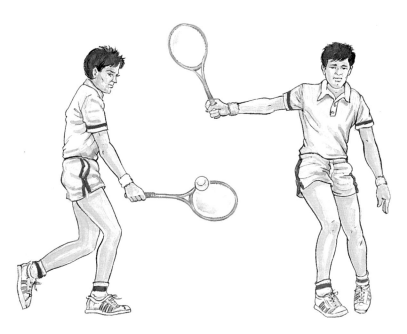

shot. Both the forehand and backhand drives are played after the ball has hit the ground.

THE DOUBLE-HANDED BACKHAND DRIVE
This shot is basically the same as the normal backhand shot

Overleaf left: *Three-times Wimbledon winner Pete Sampras defends his title at the Championship in 1996*
Overleaf right: *The inspiring Arantxa Sanchez Vicario exhibits her first-class technique by keeping her wrist firm, her back straight and her knees bent when taking a low volley*

The volley

There will be times when you see your opponent out of position and rather than give him time to recover will want to play your shot on the volley i.e. before it hits the ground. You can play volleys either with the forehand or backhand. Let's have a look at both, starting with the forehand volley.

Like the forehand and backhand drives you should be in a 'ready' position facing the net. But when you play the shot it is to the side and in front of you. You move forward on your front foot, and hold out your left arm, to help your balance. This time the racket head is held considerably higher, because it hits the ball down. As the racket is brought down you start to transfer your weight to your front foot as you move into the shot. As the ball approaches, your shoulders should be turned facing the net. The shot is played with a 'punching' motion and with a very firm wrist action. A long backswing is not needed for playing this shot. You are not applying any speed into the ball, but are using its own oncoming speed for the return volley.

The half-volley is a shot played immediately after the ball has

THE FOREHAND VOLLEY
Note how high the racket head is in the 'ready' position. You don't need a big backswing because you are only 'punching' the ball over the net. The shoulders should be square to the net at the moment of contact

bounced. Because of that, the ball is always hit close to the ground but the important thing to remember when playing the half-volley shot is to keep your back straight but allow the knees to bend. The back knee should be almost touching the ground. Provided you can get in position fast enough, you should play the shot from the side, but whatever, you must keep your eye on the ball and keep that wrist firm.

The reason for playing the half-volley is normally that you are in trouble and cannot play another shot. But you are well advised to learn how to play it, ready for the day when you will need it.

The backhand volley should, like the forehand volley, be played from a position about 3.05m (10ft) from the net for maximum efficiency and control.

You should once again adopt a 'ready' position by facing the net, moving your body towards the ball. Make sure you have adopted the backhand grip and support the racket with your left hand. The backswing is very short and when the ball is played it should be well forward of the body. The front foot will be forward to take the body-weight. The shot is played with a short 'punching' action.

The biggest error in playing the backhand volley is in allowing the wrist to slacken … I won't go on about keeping the wrist firm any more, you know all about that by now don't you?

Overleaf left: *Mary Pierce successfully plays a forehand*
Overleaf right: *Goran Ivanisevic is a talented player of immense power*

THE HALF-VOLLEY
When playing the half-volley, or any volley near to the ground, make sure your wrist is very firm, bend your knees and keep your back straight. Note the right knee in the drawing (far right) – it is almost on the ground

THE BACKHAND VOLLEY
The 'ready' position (A).
The left hand supports
the racket. As you step
on to your right foot,
support your racket
with the left hand (B).
The shot is played with
a 'punching' action, and
contact with the ball
should be just in front
of the right knee (C)

The backhand volley is a difficult stroke to play, and one which requires a lot of confidence. Inexperienced players often have trouble with this shot because they lack confidence. So: think positive; be positive!

The backhand half-volley is the same as the forehand half-volley (except that it is played with the backhand!) and the important things to remember are the firm wrist (oh no! Not again ...) and to bend the knees while keeping the back straight.

The smash

This effective and powerful shot is often a point winner. However, the biggest fault in playing the smash is taking your eye off the ball and rushing the shot. Once a novice sees the opportunity of the smash, the tendency is to get it over and done with as soon as possible. But that is a fatal error. Like any other shot, the preparation is important. After all, why should you rush just because it is likely to be a winning shot? You have a big advantage in playing the smash so don't mess it up by rushing things.

The smash should be used to counteract a lob from your opponent that has been hit short. The ideal position for the smash is again about 3.05m (10ft) from the net. It should be played from a sideways-on position. The smash is a similar shot to the service and

calls for perfect timing.

Having moved into a sideways position the free hand should be pointing out to the right. The shot should be made with full reach for maximum efficiency and, like the service, the racket should be 'thrown' up at the ball. As you take the racket back behind your head you should transfer your weight from your front to your back foot and, as you stretch into the shot, your left hand should come round and face the ball.

As you start to 'throw' the racket into the ball the shoulders should move square to the net thus allowing maximum power and the shot should be made in a downwards motion on to the ball.

It is also possible to make a backhand smash, but I don't think we will go into that at this stage of your development. It is one of the most difficult shots to play and you needn't consider playing it until you are ready for your Centre Court debut at Wimbledon …

THE SMASH
The smash demands a lot of different skills. Timing is the most important of these, but you must also keep your eye firmly on the ball, must hit the ball at the very top of your reach, and then 'throw' the racket up at the ball

The lob and the drop shot

The lob is played on the forehand or backhand but with an upward movement of the racket, the effect of which is to make the ball travel in an arc. The purpose of the lob is to play a shot over your opponent and out of his reach. Obviously, the nearer he is to the net the more chance there is of you effectively playing the lob and thereby increasing your chances of winning the point.

The drop shot is a disguised shot that just drops over the net into your opponent's half of the court. When playing it, either on the forehand or backhand, the racket face needs to be open in both cases so as to impart underspin on the ball and cause it not to bounce forwards too much when it lands. In making both shots, a good backswing, firm wrist, and 'eyes on the ball' are most important.

Summarizing: when playing the backhand or forehand drive the racket should be SWUNG through the ball; when playing the smash or serving the racket should be THROWN through the ball; and when playing the volley the racket should be PUNCHED through the ball.

Let's now have a look at the effects of spin. Once you have mastered the basic shots as already outlined you can then experiment by putting spin on the ball. Furthermore you will be able to

THE LOB
There are two forms of lob – the attacking lob and the defensive lob. The attacking lob (lower dotted line) is likely to be a winning shot whereas the defensive version of the shot (upper dotted line) is used to create time for movement into a better position on the court

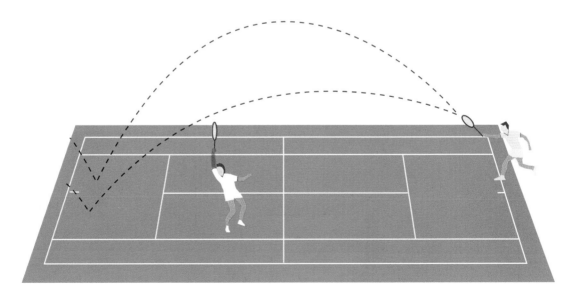

understand what happens to a ball that has spin put on it by your opponent.

There are three basic types of spin which you can put on the ball; topspin, underspin and sidespin. You can also play shots with intermediate spin between topspin and sidespin.

A ball played with topspin will dip while in flight and it will bounce higher than normal after hitting the ground. A ball hit with underspin flattens the trajectory and will 'deaden' the bounce on landing. Sidespin will cause the ball to spin away to the right or left (depending on which side you impart the spin on the ball) while in flight and upon making contact with the ground. Don't forget, if you try to volley a ball with spin on it then it may leave your racket at an 'unusual' trajectory.

Topspin is commonly used with the ground strokes when you can apply both power and spin to the ball and thus making it an effective shot if played correctly. To play topspin the racket should be swung on an upward path and with the racket face open and lifted as it makes contact with the ball.

When lobbed defensively, the ball is hit in a high trajectory, sometimes with underspin. At impact the racket face should be kept wide open and the follow-through should be high and long

When playing the attacking lob the face of the racket is lifted in an upwards movement to impart a lot of topspin on the ball

THE DROP SHOT
The key to the successful drop shot is to have the racket face open in order to impart the underspin necessary to 'check' the ball's movement once it lands on the other side of the net

To play a shot with underspin the racket face has to be open and the racket head played down through the ball at an angle. Sidespin is played similarly but the racket head is played through the ball at an angle and along the side of the ball.

Both topspin and sidespin are useful in the service. A slower service with a lot of sidespin (called slice) can cause your opponent as much trouble as a flat-hit fast service.

The secret of being able to cope with spin played against you is being able to read your opponent's next shot. It is not easy to disguise spin and you should keep your eye on the ball. If you do that correctly you will follow the path of your opponent's racket and the flight of the ball. If you correctly read your opponent's shot you can get in position to return it without any problems, whether it has spin on it or not, and make a successful return by imparting your own spin on the ball.

Tennis tactics?

Knowing where to stand within the court is important. To return the service you should stand near the baseline, depending on the amount of power your opponent puts into his first serve. If the first serve is a fault then you should move closer to the service line, but not too close, for the second serve.

Spin

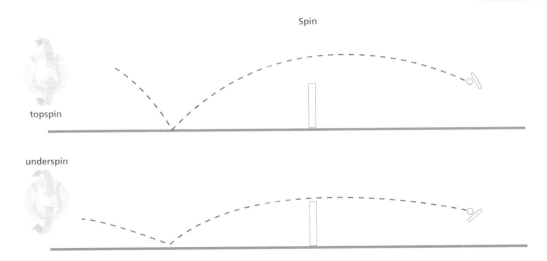

topspin

underspin

TYPES OF SPIN
Top: *The effect of topspin and subsequent bounce of the ball*
Above: *Note the low bounce of the ball played with underspin*
Right: *A ball played with sidespin (on the right-hand side of the ball) will deflect like this after bouncing in the opposite court*

sidespin

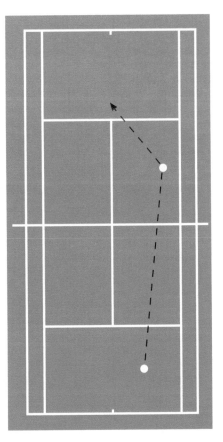

Mal Washington plays a cross-court backhand drive

After making the return, ideally you should return to a position near the centre of the court to cover any contingencies. But you mustn't be too near the baseline. Play will be dictated normally by one player taking up a position at the net and playing the volleying game. In this case you need to stand further back in your court and attempt to make the return by playing a lob, which will take him off guard and force him back into the court and away from the net.

As a novice you will be happy just to get the ball over the net and make a rally. But once you become more adept you will want to try and outwit your opponent. Brains as well as brawn help win tennis matches.

You will want to vary your shots. Play some with topspin, some with sidespin, and vary where you place them. If you place one shot deep into your opponent's court to his backhand and can play his return immediately into the opposite corner then he has to make up some ground to reach the shot ... he'll soon get tired if you can constantly play a range of shots like that. But don't forget – he can always do the same to you!

Tennis at senior level is a power game these days. The server will often put a powerful first service in and, after hitting the return of serve, will take up a position at the net ready to play a winning shot. But what happens if the receiver returns that shot ... then different tactics have to be employed.

The power game is not good enough alone to win matches: you must be able to play those deceptive cross-court shots, deep or angled shots, drop shots, and so on. This is when tennis becomes a tactical game – one player trying to outwit, as well as outpower, the other.

Before you can employ any tactics you must make sure you keep the ball in play. It may sound obvious, but often a novice will concentrate too hard on playing the 'difficult' shot, when the easy one will suffice. Try and keep your opponent behind the baseline – you have more chance of winning if you do. Don't forget, you do not have to play a winning shot to win a rally; most rallies are won through your opponent playing a 'losing' shot.

It is important that you maintain a good position on the court, and so be ready to execute your next shot. If not, it will be a good bet that the next ball that comes over the net to you will be a winner for your opponent. Often you will see players run like mad to reach a return, but they will not try and return to a good court position with the same enthusiasm. You should always get into a good position, and as quickly as possible.

You will hear the expression 'playing the percentage' a lot these days. It is a very important part of the game but, quite simply, it means playing a shot that gives you more of a chance of winning a point. Looking at it logically, if you do not put the ball back into play then you have no chance of playing a percentage whatsoever. Putting your first service into play gives you a greater percentage chance of success than relying upon your second serve. You must always put your return of serve into play; don't, and once again you have no chance of a percentage.

Always put your first volley into play – again, this gives you an advantage. And finally, if you are in doubt which shot to play, then play the one you are happiest with. It may not be a winning shot, but if there was any doubt in your mind, then it would most probably have been a losing shot anyway.

All the above should also be considered when playing the doubles game. Obviously court positions are considerably different, and it is vital that you know where your team-mate is at all times. You should work out a pre-determined plan of what part of the court each of you should take when serving or receiving. There are so many different combinations of court position in doubles play. Both players may take an attacking position at the net on either side of the court, or one may take the attacking position while the other defends at the rear of the court, and so on.

Basic tactics to remember in doubles play are: (a) it is a team game – don't forget you have a partner on court; (b) try and get to the net before your opponents; (c) keep the ball low over the net, particularly when returning service. Lobs in the doubles game are often losing strokes, because one, or both, opposing players stand a good chance of getting to the ball. Most good rallies in doubles are played when all four players are close to the net and balls are played low.

Like the singles game, it is important to win your service game, to keep the ball in play, and to play the percentage game. Weaknesses should also be exploited, just as in singles. But in doubles there will inevitably be a weak partner; his or her weaknesses should be exploited to the full.

Powerful server: Greg Rusedski finely poised to serve yet another incredibly fast ace

Useful
addresses

The Lawn Tennis Association
The Queen's Club
West Kensington
London W14 9EG
0171-381-7000

Tennis Australia
Private Bag 6060
Richmond South
Victoria 3121
Australia

British Women's Tennis Association
33 Princes Avenue
London W3 8LX
0181-993-3397

Tennis Canada
3111 Steeles Avenue West
Downsview
Ontario M3J 3H2
Canada

Czech Tennis Association
Ostrov Stvanice 38
170 00 Prague 7
C. Sprotsvaz Prague

Federation Francaise de Tennis
Stade Roland Garros
2 Avenue Gordon Bennett
75016 Paris
France

Deutscher Tennis Bund e.V.
Hallerstrasse 89
20149 Hamburg
Germany

All India Lawn Tennis Association
DLTA Tennis Complex
Africa Avenue
New Delhi 110 029
India

International Tennis Federation
Paliser Road
Baron's Court
London W14 9EN
0171–381–8060

Tennis Ireland
Argyle Square
Donnybrook
Dublin 4
Ireland

Federazione Italiana Tennis
Viale Tiziano 70
00196 Rome
Italy

New Zealand Lawn Tennis Association
PO Box 11541
Manners Street
Wellington
New Zealand

Slovak Tennis Association
Junacka 6
83280 Bratislava
Slovak Republic

The South African Tennis Union
PO Box 15978
Doornfontein
Johannesburg 2028
South Africa

Svenska Tennis Forbundet
PO Box 27915
S-115 94 Stockholm
Sweden

United States Tennis Association
70 West Red Oak Lane
White Plains
New York
NY 10604
USA

Rules clinic
index

Page numbers *in italics* indicate illustrations

index

Figures *in italics* indicate
illustrations

A Ward Lock Book • Cassell • Wellington House • 125 Strand • London WC2R 0BB

A Cassell Imprint • Copyright © Ward Lock 1998
All rights reserved. No part of this book may be reproduced or transmitted in any form or by any means,
electronic or mechanical, including photocopying, recording or any information storage and retrieval system,
without prior permission in writing from the publishers and copyright owner.

Distributed in the United States by • Sterling Publishing Co. Inc. • 387 Park Avenue South • New York NY 10016 • USA

British Library Cataloguing-in-Publication Data • A catalogue record for this book is available from the British Library

ISBN 0-7063-7715-X

Designed by Grahame Dudley Associates • Illustrations by Chris Rothero • Text revisions by Anne Pankhurst

Printed and bound in Spain by Graficromo S.A., Cordoba